The Knotties
with knots of fun

The Rescue

Co-Written by Philip Turner & Natalie Manning
Illustrated by Jesse Emmerson

Copyright © 2019 by Turner Creations Ltd.

ISBN: Softcover   9781645506232

All rights reserved. No part of this book may be reproduced or transmitted in any form or by any means, electronic or mechanical, including photocopying, recording, or by any information storage and retrieval system, without permission in writing from the copyright owner.

This is a work of fiction. Names, characters, places and incidents either are the product of the author's imagination or are used fictitiously, and any resemblance to any actual persons, living or dead, events, or locales is entirely coincidental.

Print information available on the last page

To order additional copies of this book, contact:
Matchstick Literary
1-888-306-8885
www.matchliterary.com
Orders@matchliterary.com

Turner Creations Ltd

The Rescue

At the bottom of a garden, underneath an old oak tree, stood a rickety little garden shed with its rusty tin roof flapping in the wind.

The sky was dark with clouds, and it was grumbling loudly.

Suddenly, a bolt of lightning zapped a branch! *Kaboom! Crack!*

The broken branch crashed down through the garden shed window, carrying the lightning charge to a basket full of coloured rope.

The lightning charge sent the basket and rope flying through the air, unravelling it across the workbench and knocking over a tin full of bits and bobs.

By the power of the electric lightning charge, little rope men began to form and the Knotties were brought to life! In complete amazement, they jumped to their feet and dusted down their little knot bodies.

The orange knot man smiled and reached out to shake hands with his new friend.

"Hello. I'm Will Knot. What's your name?" he asked.

"I'm What Knot. Pleased to meet you," replied the little red knot man.

All of a sudden, they heard a cry from beyond the workbench. "Help, help! *Help!*"

"It sounds like someone is in trouble," cried Will Knot.

Will Knot ran to the edge of the workbench to find another little knot man hanging by a thread over a tin of gooey green paint. "Help! I'm slipping," cried the little knot man.

As green paint bubbled and gurgled, the little knot man became more and more frightened. Then suddenly, the thread holding him started to fray.

"Arrrgh! Please don't let me fall in; I don't know how to swim!" screamed the knot man.

What Knot came rushing over to help Will Knot rescue the frightened little knot man. They both pulled with all their strength, but it was no use; he was still too heavy to lift.

"We need something to pull him up," said Will Knot.

"Look over there; let's use that elasticated strap!" suggested What Knot.

Will Knot quickly stretched out his tasselled arm as far as he could to retrieve the strap.

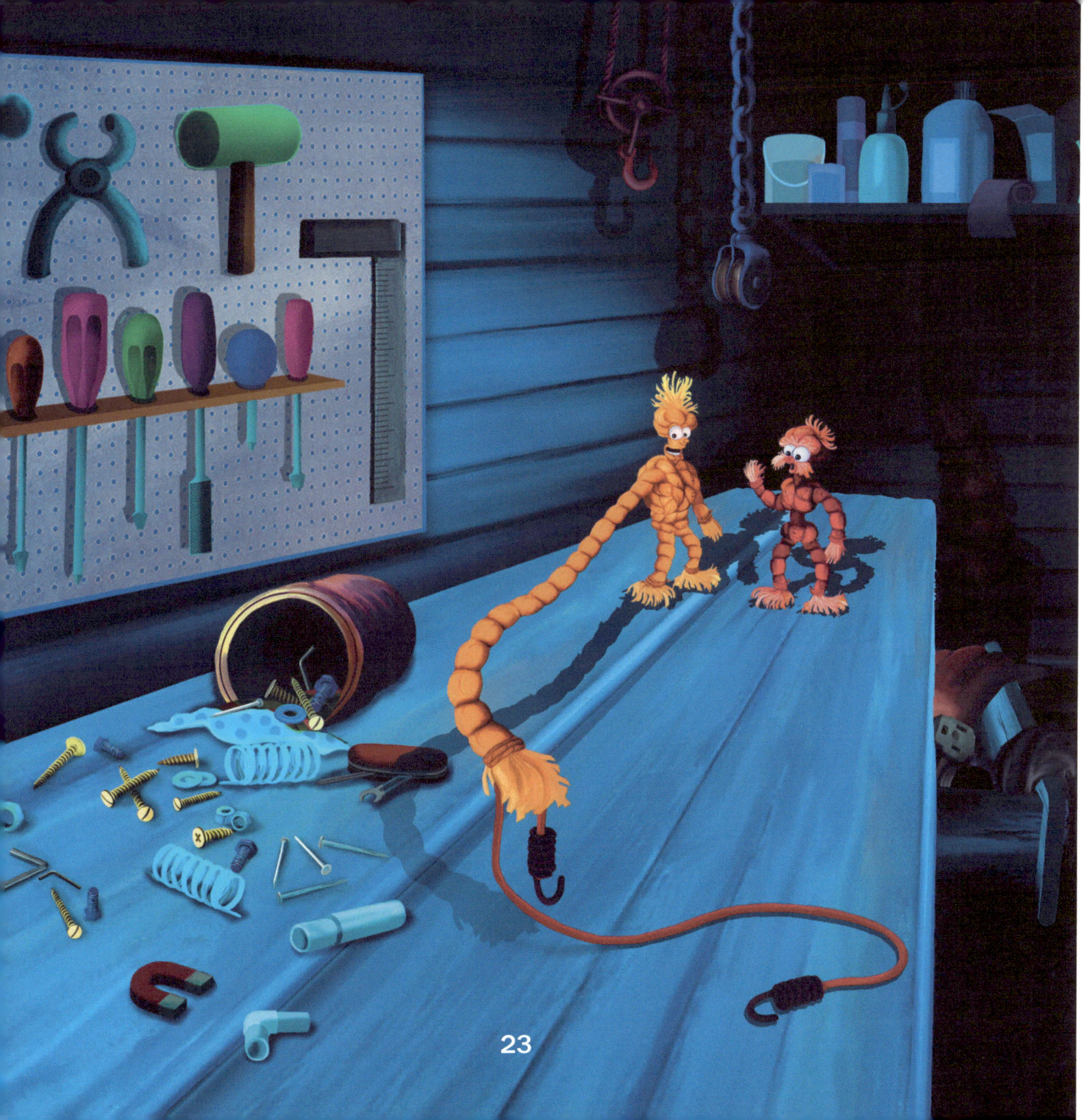

Suddenly, the little knot man's leg came loose! But as he plummeted towards the gooey paint, his tasselled foot got caught upon a rusty nail. He came so close to falling in that the tips of his looped hair dipped into the paint.

"Noooooo, not my yellow hair!" he cried.

"We need to move faster; we are running out of time!" shouted What Knot.

Will Knot looked up and around the shed for a way to hook up the elasticated strap.

"Look up there!" Will Knot pointed. "I'll attach one end of the strap to that pulley."

"Good idea! I'll find something to help secure the other end," replied What Knot.

What Knot grabbed a magnet that had fallen out of the tin, placing it around his waist, and then secured it with a threaded nut.

Will Knot climbed up from the workbench and rigged the elasticated strap to the pulley.

What Knot secured the other end to his new magnet belt.

"Hold on—we're coming to save you!" called Will Knot.

The little knot man couldn't hold on any longer; the thread on his tasselled foot snapped.

"Aargh!" cried the little knot man as he fell towards the open tin of paint.

With one fell swoop, Will Knot caught him in the nick of time.

The little knot man was relieved. He shouted, "Thank you, thank you!"

Will Knot waved to What Knot to pull them up to safety.

"Wow. That was close," said the little knot man as they landed on the workbench. He shook hands with his rescuers. "Hi. I'm Why Knot. Thank you for coming to my rescue."

"Lucky we had these useful tools to get you out of trouble," said What Knot.

Gathering up their new favourite gadgets, Will Knot stood up tall and proud. "Now that we have our bits and bobs, we are ready for our next adventure. Then together we will have *knots of fun!*"

www.ingramcontent.com/pod-product-compliance
Lightning Source LLC
Chambersburg PA
CBHW041117070526
44584CB00002B/201